Secrets of Successful House Parties:
Effectively Raise Money/Awareness or Mobilize for Action

Grace Concepts
1165 Pennsylvania St., #2C
Denver, CO 80203

ISBN: 1-4196-5216-8
Library Of Congress Control Number: 2007900311

To order additional copies, please contact
Amazon.com

Table of Contents

Preface

Over the years House Parties have become a popular and effective tool to raise money/awareness and to mobilize for action. When organized correctly, with sufficient time for preparation and adequate direction, House Parties can be quite successful. Unfortunately, guidance for hosting parties has not kept pace with their use. Hosts are often left without adequate direction, and nonprofit staff or volunteers too frequently aren't familiar with the essential details.

This manual is a guide for nonprofits and hosts, and may be modified to fit specific styles and needs. However, do not underestimate the time required to organize, execute, and follow up on a successful House Party. Hosting a successful House Party depends largely on good communication between organization staff and the host(s). The fewer assumptions and misunderstandings there are, the better the outcome.

Please let me know how this manual is helpful and how it can be enhanced. Go to: http://www.graceconcepts.com/ and contact me. It is my goal to keep improving this publication so it will continue to be a helpful guide.

A note of thanks to Lois Hart for inspiration; Cathy Kuykendall for ideas and initial editing; Bruce M. Abrams, Dr. Juan Jover, and Dr. Ken Ahonen for encouragement and suggestions; Phoebe Lawrence for her generosity of time, talent, and knowledge; all the donors and experienced hosts for offering suggestions; and David Westman for illustrations and layout. As with House Parties, this manual truly is a team effort.

Introduction

The manual is in action-bullet format for easy reading and implementation. It offers practical suggestions for developing successful House Parties. My goal is to minimize the amount of time and effort you expend and maximize the return on those efforts.

There are specific tasks for the organization staff/volunteers and others for the host. One of the first secrets to successful House Parties is for your organization to set policies for hosting events and clearly outline guidelines for potential host(s). Some of these guidelines may include: maximum dollars spent on hosting an event, ticket prices, geographic area covered, number of people attending, etc. As the name House Party implies, these events will be held in someone's private home. There are psychological advantages to having people come into someone's home – a private environment. If you choose to hold a House Party in a more public venue, be very clear about your reasons. There will be a different 'feel' when held in a public venue, less intimacy with attention possibly being diverted by the surroundings. This less intimate location may affect the outcome, positively or negatively, depending on planning and organizing.

Included on page 42 is an easy-to-use checklist for your organization and another on page 44 for hosts.

If your organization plans to hold multiple House Parties at the same time, it is important to organize even more efficiently. This manual will guide you through the important specifics. In order to coordinate effectively, it is helpful to use your web site or another web-based organizing tool, as well as blast E-mails to all participants to ensure everyone receives the same correct and timely information.

Notes

Secret #1: Identify Your Goal

Know your goal. You cannot serve more than one 'master' at a time. It is either to raise money, to raise awareness, or to mobilize for action, that takes the lead. Occasionally you may use House Parties to thank volunteers or donors. Modify the suggestions in this manual accordingly.

Whether your organization's House Parties are for fundraising, awareness-raising, or mobilization, the decisions must be linked to organizational planning and goals.

Raise Money

How much do you want to raise at this event?

At what level are people expected to give?

> ★ It's best not to ask for too much or too little. Your invitation list should be in line with what people can/will give. Don't mix 'high dollar' and 'low dollar' at the same event. If the difference between the two is $300 or more, offer something special (e.g., pre-event reception) to the high-dollar donors.

For raising money, the dollar amount brought in by the event is what determines success. Money received prior to the event, as a result of the invitation, during or shortly after the event counts toward success. Receiving money prior to the event is preferable. The number of people in attendance is not the most important element at fundraising events. Money raised is.

Decide whether people will be asked to pay prior to coming, be asked to give at the event, or both.

You may want to ask people to contribute less than you know they are capable of giving if they are new to your organization. Once they have given, you can work with them to increase their next gift.

Ask 'key' donors to offer a challenge at the event. Prior to the event, raise X amount of money to be matched dollar-for-dollar or with a certain number of 'new' donors to your organization. You may think of other creative ways to challenge people to give at the event. It's a bonus, but not a necessity, if the donor making the challenge is present and offers the challenge in person.

Have people in the audience who are already committed, give X amount that night to 'prime the pump' with contribution amounts at a high level, a match of other contributions at a set level or a challenge, immediately following the 'ask.' This gets the giving started.

Notes

Raise Awareness

To raise awareness, the number of people in attendance is what determines success.

As with raising money, geography is generally not an issue for raising awareness. You want your organization's message spread far and wide unless there is a specific, limited geographic region it serves. Even then it's possible to gain support beyond your borders.

You can and should ask for money at these events (see Secret #5: Ask for the Money). However, getting your organization's mission and message in front of as many people as possible is the goal. Any money raised is icing on the cake whereas at fundraising events, money raised is the cake!

Mobilize for Action

For mobilizing people to action, the number of commitments to action is what determines success.

Geography may be important when mobilizing for action. Focus your efforts on people in a certain area if they are going to speak directly with others. People like hearing from their neighbors more than they do people from 'out of town.' Focus on people who live in specific voter districts if you are mobilizing to contact elected officials. It's best to have people contact an official from her/his district.

You can have envelopes at the sign-in table for contributions and/or a 'bowl' in which people can put money. (Always 'prime the pump' with some $5s and $20s before people arrive.) The 'ask' for money at these events should be very soft. Action is what you're after.

The invitation list should include people you know who are already committed to your organization or the action for which you're organizing. Encourage those invited to bring others with them.

Have a very clear, concise, and well-thought-out plan of action. Know exactly what you need and don't need for successful mobilization before holding an event.

Notes

Secret #2: Timing Is Critical

During what part of the year does your organization hold House Parties? Take into account weather, vacations, school schedules, etc.

Select Day and Time

★ Know your constituency. What time of day and day of week work best?

★ What works best for the host(s)?

★ Check community calendars for possible conflicts.

★ Schedule no more than two hours for each gathering.

Secret #3: Know Your Host
(See Appendix: Questions to Ask Potential Hosts)

Select potential hosts for their particular strength in fundraising, awareness-raising, or mobilization. Not everyone is equally suited. Determine who is best for which goal. It may help to ask them directly.

Identify Strengths and Limitations

★ Be realistic about how much time the host can/will devote to this event (i.e., preparation and follow-up). It may be a high priority for your organization, perhaps not for the host.

★ Use the host's strengths to your organization's advantage (e.g., knowledge, experience, connections, wealth level, status, beautiful home that others will want to see, etc.).

★ Compensate for the host's weaknesses with other volunteers/staff.

★ Invite friends/family of the host. It's all about relationships, and these are the strongest ones.

★ If the event is for raising money, work with the host on her/his invitation list for invitees' ability to contribute at an appropriate level. You don't want to ask someone who can give at a high level to give at a significantly lower level.

Involve Host in Planning

★ No one likes being 'told' what to do – get buy-in early.

★ All aspects of planning the event (invitations, publicity, public speaking, asking for money, follow-up, etc.) are important to the host.

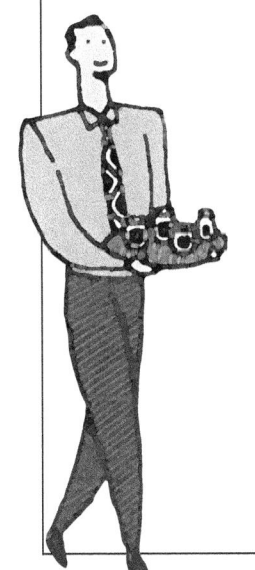

★ Your organization always maintains control within specified parameters. Work with the host as you guide the event.

★ Let the host know up front what the expectations are for the event. If it is a fundraiser, how much money must be raised? If it's an awareness-raising or mobilizing event, what is the minimum number of individuals needed at the event to assure success, and what is the spending limit (i.e., budget)?

Ask for the Money

★ What is the host's comfort level in asking for money?

★ Has the host asked for money before? Was she/he successful? Through invitations? One-on-one 'asks'? 'Asks' to a group?

★ Review what it is you want the host(s) to say. Practice, if necessary. The 'ask' for money is one of the most important elements in fundraising. It can mean the difference between success and failure. Even at awareness-raising events, there must be a strong, appropriate 'ask.'

★ Do not be afraid to have someone else do the 'ask' and have the host welcome and thank the guests only. The most important aspect in choosing the person is to ensure that she/he is the strongest and most appropriate one.

Host Committees

★ Expectations of Host Committee members

    ★ Host Committee names are used to generate increased interest in the event.

    ★ Members are expected to give and raise certain pre-determined dollar amounts for fundraising events.

    ★ Members are expected to invite a pre-determined number of individuals for awareness-raising and mobilizing parties.

    ★ Members are expected to attend the event.

    ★ Members must send out appropriate and timely thank-you notes (see Secret #6: Follow-up).

★ Cautions when using Host Committees

    ★ Host Committee members too frequently do not give or raise money.

Notes

★ Increased organizing, record-keeping, and follow-up are required to keep Host Committee members informed, on task, and thanked. It's important to:

> ★ Maintain accurate records for each Host Committee member. These records must track the number of invitations issued by each individual, the amount of money directly attributable to the member, individuals attending the event as a result of each member's efforts, and appropriate and timely thank-you notes sent.

> ★ Repeatedly inquire about the status of Host Committee members' invitations issued and responses received.

★ Host Committee members often do not attend the event.

★ Host Committee members frequently do not send out thank-you notes in a timely manner, if at all.

Secret #4: Responsibilities/Assignments Are Key

Host Responsibilities (see Appendix: Timeline)

Select day and time collaboratively with the organization's staff.

Establish an invitation list.

> ★ Be sure the majority of invitees are 'new to the organization.' This helps bring in new money and new energy.

Issue invitations (see Secret #5: Invitations).

Follow up invitations with a phone call.

> ★ Your rate of attendance will be enhanced with a follow-up phone call to all or at least a select number of invited individuals.

Have as many people as possible send in money prior to all fundraising events. This increases the likelihood that the event will be successful and is a good way to sustain/increase momentum. Make sure information for giving ahead of time is clear on each invitation.

Plan and provide refreshments within parameters set by the organization.

Ensure adequate seating/space for all attendees.

Provide sufficient space and equipment for entertainment, if any.

Notes

Provide a sign-in table at the door and a trash receptacle. Table must be large enough to hold name tags and up to three contact information sheets (see Secret #5: Capture Contact Information).

Ensure that all guests are introduced to each other as they arrive.

Introduce staff/board of the organization to all guests as they arrive and throughout the event.

Have something on which the speakers can stand. Be sure it is steady and safe. This is especially important if the guests will be standing during presentations by board/staff and the person asking for money. The speakers must be visible to everyone.

Provide microphones and loud speakers if necessary for the particular venue.

If a video presentation is part of the program, provide monitors that are visible to everyone.

Tape down all cords to lessen the possibility of someone tripping.

Send out timely and appropriate thank-you notes (see Secret #6: Follow-up).

Organization Responsibilities

Identify appropriate host(s).

Select day and time collaboratively with host.

Review timeline with host.

Identify desired outcome (i.e., money, awareness or mobilization).

Review financial constraints, if any, and reporting expectations with the host.

- ★ Budget (see Secret #7: Expenses)
- ★ Contributions
    - ★ What contact information must be captured for each contributor?
    - ★ From what individuals and/or corporations/unions will your organization not accept contributions, if any?
- ★ Entertainment
- ★ Refreshments

Review invitee list with host; add to the list as desired.

Provide script or wording for flyers or invitations (written or verbal).

Notes

Review refreshments to be served with the host.

Stay in touch with the host to ensure invitations have been issued and follow-up calls made. Contact the host every few days to share information and ensure they are doing what they said they would, when they said they would (see Appendix: House Party Planning Timeline and Checklist).

> ★ Do not assume that all necessary steps are being accomplished by the host. *Stay on top of it all.*

Receive RSVPs for event, electronically, via phone and/or mail. Your organization wants to capture all the contact information, and this helps ensure that you will. In addition, receiving RSVPs lets you know how well the invitations are being received and provides you with an accurate up-to-date number of responses.

Identify the person who will speak on behalf of your organization.

Let the host know who will attend and speak on behalf of the organization. This should also be clear on the invitations.

Draft remarks for the speaker.

Check in periodically (see Appendix: Timeline) to update the host on status of RSVPs.

Create appropriate contact sheets (see Secret #5: Event Logistics).

Provide name tags and Sharpies. (Never use pens or pencils for name tags because they are too difficult to read.)

Provide sign-in sheets and pens (see Event Logistics: Contact Information).

Provide handouts.

> ★ Self-addressed contribution envelopes
>
> ★ Brochures
>
> ★ Pins
>
> ★ Whatever materials your organization has

Timeline

Use the timeline provided in this manual. Organization staff fill out the forms with appropriate dates and give a copy to the host (see Appendix: Timeline).

Notes

Staff/Volunteer Participation

Dress appropriately for the event. Business casual to dressy, never too casual. How board, staff and volunteers dress reflects, for good or ill, on the organization.

Board, staff and volunteers must 'work' throughout the event. They are each there as ambassadors. Their responsibility starts when they arrive and does not end until they leave.

Administrative staff/volunteers have the following responsibilities:

★ Create name tags for each guest. Do this ahead of time, if possible, with extra blank tags for those who did not RSVP. Whether on the computer or by hand, always print the first name in LARGE bold letters with the last name somewhat smaller. It is important that names be easily read from a distance.

★ Capture complete contact information (i.e., name, mailing address, phone numbers, E-mail address).

★ Hand out flyers, brochures, etc.

★ Introduce guests to each other and to the organization board/staff as they arrive.

★ Talk with guests.

Responsibilities of the speaker assistant are to:

★ Stay with the speaker throughout the event.

★ Take adequate notes of pertinent conversations for follow-up.

★ Introduce the speaker to as many guests as possible.

★ Watch the time and keep the speaker on time.

★ Be prepared to cut off questions during Q & A if the crowd is restless or time has run out.

Early on, your organization must set parameters and expectations for board/staff/volunteer participation in events. These parameters may change along the way.

★ For fundraising events.

★ Establish a guideline that outlines the minimum amount to be raised to require board member attendance. These are internal expectations and should guide host selection.

Notes

Use your board members wisely by respecting their volunteer time. The executive director and/or senior staff should attend all events.

★ Set a policy about volunteer participation. Are they expected to contribute financially? If so, tell them ahead of time. How many are needed? Be sure they know their roles and are 'working' the entire time.

★ For awareness-raising events.

★ Set a policy for the minimum number of people you expect at these events to ensure that it is time- and cost-effective. Again, use staff and board members' time wisely.

★ Make these expectations clear to all potential hosts.

Speaker

Make sure the person speaking on behalf of your organization is a good public speaker, knows the organization extremely well, and is comfortable answering questions. Include the individual's name on the invitation if she/he is well known.

She/he must:

★ Show up on time.

★ Have appropriate remarks prepared.

★ Deliver remarks.

★ Leave as scheduled.

If the speaker is not there in person, will she/he be there via:

★ Speaker phone?

★ DVD?

★ Video conference?

★ Web cast?

For these options ensure that appropriate technology is set up and in working order, including being audible and visible to all. Work well in advance on this with the host.

Notes

Secret #5: Success Is in the Details of Event Logistics

Invitations

Invitations are more likely to be read if they are sent with the return address of someone the invitee knows or respects rather than with your organization's address.

★ You can add a host's name to your organization's return address and increase positive response rates.

Hand address envelopes when at all possible.

As a guideline, you must invite at least twice as many people as you hope will attend.

Invitations must include:

★ Reason for the event (i.e., 100th anniversary of your organization, special project, general support for the organization, etc.).

★ Host name.

★ Host Committee names.

★ Date, time, location.

★ Name and title of the person speaking if it will increase contributions/attendance.

★ RSVP information and date by which it must be received.

★ Cost.

　　★ Must the money be sent prior to the event? Will it be collected at the door? Will you have a 'suggested donation' only? (Suggested donation means people don't have to contribute in order to attend.)

　　★ Are there various financial levels? Host? Special guests? Couples? How much for each?

★ Make checks payable to: (organization name).

★ How to contribute electronically, if possible. Include your web address.

★ Name of person to contact, phone number, or E-mail address for further information.

Notes

Organization staff must be very clear with the host(s) about who is sending invitations, by what date they must be sent, and what medium will be used. Always use fonts that are easily readable – nothing fancy. It is more important for them to be easily read, rather than be extra fancy.

- ★ E-mail
    - ★ Text is written by organization staff.
    - ★ Invitation is sent from the host/committee or your organization and is personalized as much as possible.
- ★ Phone
    - ★ Script is provided by organization staff.
    - ★ Calls are made by the host/committee.
- ★ Snail mail
    - ★ Text is written by organization staff.
    - ★ Sent with the host/committee return address.
    - ★ Use first-class stamps. People are more likely to open envelopes that are hand-addressed and stamped. Opening the envelope is the first step in getting them to the event.
- ★ Flyers
    - ★ Designed and written by organization staff.
    - ★ May be copied by the host/committee for distribution.
    - ★ E-mail.
    - ★ Snail mail.
    - ★ May also be distributed, if paper, by organization.

The host/committee and/or organization staff/volunteers always make follow-up phone calls to entire invitation list or key people on the list, two days to one week prior to the event.

Save-the-date notices (cards or E-mail) may be used when the event is more than five weeks away. This simply gives a 'heads up' to people that the event is coming up and that they will be receiving an invitation.

- ★ Your organization must be ready to receive RSVPs and contributions for the event when the save-the-date notices are sent.

Notes

Contact Information

Have separate sign-in sheets for:

★ Those who have pre-paid. (This ensures they don't have to wait in a line with those who have not yet paid.)

★ Those who have not paid.

★ Elected officials, if any. You really don't need their contact information for follow-up, so you don't want them on the general contact sheets.

Be sure to let people know that their contact information will be used by the host organization. Include a system that allows them to 'opt out' if they don't want to receive notices, etc.

Entertainment

Use as background while people arrive and after program has concluded.

May be featured as part of the program.

★ Timing is critical. The speaker should follow entertainment so that momentum for giving/supporting is not lost.

★ Entertainment must last no more than 20-30 minutes.

Refreshments

Serve as people arrive.

At conclusion of program, encourage people to help themselves.

Agenda

Outline the agenda for the event ahead of time. Give a copy to all involved (i.e., organization staff/volunteers, hosts, speakers, etc.).

Ensure that everyone is in the room and away from the food and drinks for the program.

Welcome, Introductions, and Thank-yous

★ Who will do these?

★ If the host is not comfortable speaking publicly, ask someone who is. Preferably you know first-hand that the person is a good speaker.

Notes

★ Suggest remarks or write them out completely. This helps prevent 'missed' opportunities.

★ Ask everyone to silence their cell phones and pagers.

★ Ensure that all individuals to be thanked or recognized are on a list for the person doing the thanking. Keep introductions to a minimum. If there are elected officials there, introduce them collectively. Remember – this is an event for YOUR organization. (Hosts and organization must work together on this.)

Content Speech

★ Board/staff if present – in person or via some medium.

    ★ Must be prepared – keep it concise and short (15 minutes max).

    ★ Must talk about your organization's mission, successes, and challenges – not money! That will come later and from someone else.

    ★ Use visuals when possible. Always use positive reflections of your work, never the dark side (e.g., for animal rights, don't show animals being abused – show the cute ones, the ones that will be received well, the successes, the hopes, the vision).

    ★ Take questions for a limited time if the speaker is present electronically or in person.

★ When using technology, make sure everyone can see and/or hear. Ensure that the speaker phone is adequate, the monitor large enough, etc.

★ It is better NOT to use technology than to have it be inadequate or malfunctioning.

Ask for the Money

★ Who will 'ask'? *Not the executive director or other staff.* People who have already given are the best askers if comfortable in front of a crowd. They are good examples and can invite others to join them.

    ★ Be prepared. Organization staff must work with the person who will do the 'ask' to ensure all important points are covered.

Notes

★ Has the person ever asked for money before? Was she/he comfortable? Successful?

★ Review what it is you want the person asking to say. Give her/him a script or at least talking points. Practice, if necessary.

★ Frequently it's best to have someone other than the host do the 'ask.' This allows her/him to focus on introductions and to say thank-you in addition to the other details of hosting.

★ Make sure the 'ask' contains information that 'tugs at the heart strings' as well as offers logic. This reaches everyone and allows people to know that they are making the 'right' decision by supporting your organization for emotional and logical reasons.

★ Let people know how they can give – pledge cards being passed, baskets being passed, credit cards accepted, etc. Encourage all to give while they are there. Collect pledge cards at the time or at the door as people leave. Let everyone know the process and make sure you have adequate staff/ volunteers to keep the process going.

★ Ensure that the person doing the 'ask' is comfortable with silence. Keep the momentum going, but allow enough silence that participants will break it with a donation.

★ Possibilities (see Secret #1: Goals)

★ Have a 'plant' in the audience, someone prepared to give at the highest level you believe is possible for the specific event. Offer a challenge contribution (e.g., I'll write a $400 check if X number of others will do the same tonight).

★ Offer a match (e.g., I'll contribute $50 for every other $50 or more donation up to $X tonight).

★ Keep a running tally of money pledged/received. Include dollars/pledges received prior to but as a result of the event, at the door and during the 'ask.'

Notes

★ Announce these along the way as a way to stimulate additional and/or increased gifts/pledges.

★ Invite others to host an event.

★ Gather names and contact information immediately. Don't wait for them to sign up after it's all over.

The Close

★ Host, or selected person, thank people for coming, encourage them to stay and talk with the individuals from the organization. Remind them that pledge cards and/or contributions will continue to be collected and someone will be at the door.

★ Make sure someone, staff/volunteer, is at the door to thank them for coming even if you aren't collecting pledges/contributions there.

Notes

Secret #6: The Event Is Not Over Until Follow-up Is Complete

Within 24 Hours

★ Thank-you note, snail mail, to the host(s). This should be a personalized card from the executive director or board chair with or without a phone call.

★ Thank-you notes, calls, E-mails to all who gave money or time. The notes must include specifics of what you're thanking them for (e.g., exact dollar amount, specific volunteer activity, etc.). Do not ask them for more money or time in this thank-you.

★ For money received at any event.

> ★ Personal thank-you to those who contributed before or at the event, from the executive director or board chair.

>> ★ Snail mail, E-mail, or phone depending on amounts given. The decision is to be made by organization.

Within 48 Hours

★ Thank-you to all who attended but did not contribute or sign up for action. Encourage them to give or participate in mobilization.

> ★ From host and/or organization staff/volunteer.

> ★ Via E-mail or phone.

Within One Week

★ Contact all who were invited and did not attend. For example, "I'm sorry you weren't able to attend the X event on X date. I'd still like for you to participate in this very important organization. To make a financial contribution or to volunteer, go to (web address). Please let me know if you have questions. I'd be happy to answer them." (Be sure to leave your E-mail address or phone number.)

> ★ Host and/or organization.

> ★ E-mail or phone.

★ Organization staff and host debrief.

★ Make adjustments as necessary for improving next event.

Notes

Secret #7: Expenses Are Kept
to an Appropriate Minimum
(See Appendix: Sample Budget)

Share the budget with the host prior to any planning. Make sure the hosts understand the organization's parameters. Money spent on the event is money that will not go to your organization. Therefore, use it wisely.

★ Sharing the budget up front gives hosts a realistic guideline for the House Party.

★ Include legal restraints, if any, especially for politically focused events.

37

APPENDIX

About the Author

Ms. Gracey formed Grace Concepts in 2002. Since then she has worked with numerous organizations nationally including a two-year contract with the Democratic National Committee (DNC) where she served as Director of the Gay and Lesbian Leadership Council, the most successful fundraising council at the DNC. Prior to starting Grace Concepts, Ms. Gracey served as director of donor resources for the Gill Foundation (Denver, CO), guiding philanthropy education programs for independent major donors nationwide. She also led fundraising and board development workshops for nonprofits across the country. Previously she was programs director for The Women's Foundation of Colorado. Here she established grant-application and grant-review procedures, identified programs for funding, and worked to establish more equal partnerships between the foundation and nonprofit organizations. From 1993 to 1995, Ms. Gracey was chief of staff to Swanee Hunt, U. S. Ambassador to Austria. Ms. Gracey also served Hunt in the United States for several years as chief of staff for Hunt's political and business activities. Ms. Gracey oversaw a professionally diverse staff and guided grant-making initiatives for The Hunt Alternatives Fund in mental health, housing and homelessness, the expansion of reproductive options for women. and poverty programs.

Her professional experience also includes directing grassroots advocacy efforts, managing high-level social policy initiatives, and developing programs and direct services. Ms. Gracey has a broad background in politics. She served as scheduler for a Colorado governor where she developed and implemented extensive administrative and programmatic reforms. Ms. Gracey served for six years in the Mennonite Voluntary Service. She helped to create and operate programs for people experiencing homelessness. She founded and directed a national advocacy organization aimed at reform of the criminal justice system. In addition, she worked with people experiencing major mental illnesses at a community mental health center.

Ms. Gracey has participated in several advanced leadership programs. She is a graduate of the Denver Community Leadership Forum, a program of the University of Colorado Graduate School of Public Affairs. Ms. Gracey was a Fellow at the 1994 Salzburg Seminar's 'Non Governmental Organizations in Democratic Societies,' which was attended by people from more than 35 countries. She has participated in several educational courses including: *Training in Motion, Instructional Design, 25 Creative Ways to Add Excitement to Your Training, Co-Active Coaching, Decision Making and Conflict Management, Mastering Meetings for Results, and Myers Briggs Type Inventory Qualifying Program.*

Ms. Gracey's leadership skills developed through a variety of challenging positions: in the public and private sectors, as a donor, an entrepreneur, a management executive, a volunteer, a team member, and as a consultant. She has an unyielding commitment to help build strong communities through partnerships among government, nonprofits, philanthropists, and corporate entities. She is formally educated in psychology.

Notes

Questions to Ask Potential Hosts

1. Have you ever hosted a House Party? Was it for raising money/awareness or for mobilizing people to action?

2. If you have, what was the outcome? What was your experience? (How was success defined? Was it reached? What would you do differently?)

3. Do you want to raise money/awareness or help mobilize people for a particular action? (See Secret #1: Goals.) Be sure the staff person knows what is most needed by your organization so she/he can make suggestions to potential hosts. Work to reach compromise that works for both. Be honest about minimums needed (money or people) for an event.

4. Do you have a date in mind? Be clear about needing to check with the executive director and/or board members who will attend and for any potential conflicts. Best to get three or four dates and confirm with potential host as quickly as possible.

5. How much money do you believe you can raise at this event? Or, how many individuals do you think will attend? Note to organization: Know your minimum expectations. People are often unrealistic about the numbers – money and people. Some will high ball; others will low ball. You should talk further with potential hosts to determine which may be true, if either.

6. About how many people will be on your invitation list? Many potential hosts are surprised to find that they are expected to provide the invitation list. Be sure to make this clear from the start.

HOUSE PARTY PLANNING TIMELINE CHECKLIST

Time until/ after party	Date	Activity	Responsible	Completion date/person
6-12 months out		Each year decide the role House Parties will play in the organization's fundraising, awareness-raising, and/or mobilization activities.	Organization	
6-12 months out		Decide fundraising policies that affect House Parties (see Introduction).	Organization	
6-12 months out		Decide who in organization will take lead (HPD) and oversee organizing, execution, and follow-up for the various types of House Parties.	Organization	
6-12 months out		Identify logical potential hosts for each type of House Party.	Organization	
6 months out		Notify web people that events will be happening -- prepare for on-line registration, notification, RSVP, etc.	HPD	
6 months out		Contact potential hosts - note their availability, limits, etc. (see Questions, page 41).	HPD	
6 months out		Decide if/where to post events, all or selective ones (organizations, web sites, political entities, etc.).	Organization	
3 months out		Meet with hosts and give them an overview of what's expected. Decide if Host Committee is required/desired. Work with hosts on the following: (1) Set goals for house party (see Identify Your Goals, page 5). (2) Set criteria for participation. (3) Identify Host Committee. (4) Establish logistical commitments: (a) invitation lists; (b) save the date cards; (c) invitations -- print, E-mail, phone; (d) Host Committee invitation and follow-up; (e) caterer; (f) entertainment. (5) Develop budget. (6) Identify potential speakers. (7) Select who will do the 'ask' (see Ask for the Money, page 29).	HPD/Host	
3 months out		If there's a planning committee, meet with them to do above.	HPD/Committee	
3 months out		Establish invitation list.	HPD/Host/Committee	
3 months out		If save-the-date notices are going out, identify how many will receive them. If printed, design and send to printer or develop for E-mail distribution.	HPD	
6-10 weeks out		Send save-the-date cards/E-mail.	HPD	
10 weeks out		If printed invitations are needed, identify count, design, and send to printer.	HPD/Host/Committee	
5 weeks out		Send printed invitations.	HPD/Host/Committee	
3 weeks out		Send E-mail invitations.	HPD/Host/Committee	

HOUSE PARTY PLANNING TIMELINE CHECKLIST

Time until/after party	Date	Activity	Responsible	Completion date/person
2 weeks out		Printed materials/packets prepared: brochures, bumper stickers, T-shirts, buttons, bio, etc.	HPD	
Ongoing		Reservations confirmed via web/phone/E-mail.	HPD	
Ongoing		Respond with an E-mail to each RSVP received, whether 'will attend' or 'will not attend.'		
2 days - 1 week out		Call all invited. It's best if caller is person with closest relationship with invitee. Second best is if calls are made by organization staff/volunteers.	HPD/Host/Committee	
1 week out		Prepare appropriate contact sheets.	HPD	
1 week out		Supplies mailed to host if out of town. Boxed to take if in town. name tags, sign-up sheets, scissors, tape, gift for hosts/speakers, pens, Sharpies, stapler.	HPD	
1 week out		Confirm RSVP number with host for caterer. Deduct 15-25% for no-shows.	HPD	
1-2 days before		Prepare speaking points and overall agenda for board member, volunteer, or staff.	HPD	
1-2 days before		Assign an assistant to board member/ED for event.	HPD	
EVENT				
Within 24 hours after event		Send thank-yous from board chair/ED to host/committees.	HPD	
Within 24 hours after event		Send thank-yous from board chair/ED to all who contributed or signed up for action depending on the type of event, whether they attended or not.	HPD/Host/Committee	
Within 48 hours after event		Send thank-yous to all who attended but did not contribute or sign up for action. Encourage their participation.	HPD/Host/Committee	
Within 1 week		Contact all those who were invited but did not attend, contribute, or sign up for action. Encourage them to do so.	HPD/Host/Committee	
Within 1 week		Organization staff and host de-brief event. Note changes to make.	HPD/Host ·	
Within 1 week		Ask host to serve as advisor to other hosts.	HPD	
Ongoing		Insert hosts into process as new ones are identified.	HPD	
HPD = Organization's House Party Director				

HOST TIMELINE

Time until and after party	Date	Activity	Responsible	Completion date/person
3 months out		Meet with organization staff and they'll give you an overview of what's expected. Decide if Host Committee is required/desired (see Secret #3: Know Your Host: Host Committees, page 11). Work with the organization's staff on the following: (1) Set goals for house party (see Secret #1: Identify Your Goals, page 5). (2) Set criteria for participation. (3) Identify Host Committee, if desired. (4) Establish logistical commitments: (a) invitation lists; (b) save-the-date cards; (c) invitations -- print, E-mail, phone; (d) Host Committee invitation and follow-up; (e) caterer; (f) entertainment. (5) Develop budget. (6) Identify potential speakers. (7) Select who will do the 'ask' (see Ask for the Money, page, 29)	HPD/Host	
3 months out		Select date and time for event.	HPD/Host	
3 months out		Establish invitation list and provide to organization.	HPD/Host/Committee	
10 weeks out		If save-the-date notices are going out organization will get it to you (print, electronic, or phone script). Send/call.	Host/Committee	
6 weeks out		Send printed invitations if necessary.		
5 weeks out		Send E-mail invitations or phone invitations.		
3-6 weeks out		Engage caterer and entertainment.		
2-4 weeks out		Plan for 'at the event' items below.		
1 week out		Call through invitation list(s). Call all on list(s) or at least a select number of individuals. This works best if caller is person with closest relationship with invitee. Second best is if calls are made by organization staff/volunteers.	HPD/Host/Committee	
1 week out		Organization will provide RSVP numbers. Deduct 15-25% for no-shows when planning food/beverages. This is generally the case unless there is a 'big celebrity' present.		
At the event		Provide adequate/appropriate refreshments. Be aware of the amount you can spend.		
At the event		Ensure adequate seating/space for all attendees.		
At the event		Provide sign-in table at door for name tags, sign-in sheet, and a trash receptacle (see Host Responsibilities, page 13).		
At the event		Ensure that everyone is introduced when they arrive.		
At the event		Introduce board member/ED and/or staff to all as everyone arrives.		
Within 48 hours after event		Send personalized thank-yous to speakers and close friends.	Host/Committee	
Within 1 week		Contact those who attended but didn't contribute or sign up for action. Invite them to do so.	Host/Committee	
Within 1 week		Contact those who were invited but did not attend – encourage them to contribute or get involved.	Host/Committee	

HOUSE PARTY SAMPLE BUDGET

Item	Estimate	Actual	Difference
Save-the-Date Notices			
Invitations			
Refreshments			
Entertainment			
Thank-You Cards			
Postage			
Printed Ads			
Audio Visual Needs (i.e., sound system, visuals, etc.)			
Collateral Materials (i.e., brochures, self-addressed envelopes, buttons, etc.)			
Guest Speaker Expenses (honorarium, travel, hotel, food, etc.)			
Total Cost			

Grace Concepts

COACHING

Increase Fundraising Effectiveness

Strategic Planning

Donor and Volunteer Stewardship

Clarify Board/Committee Roles and Responsibilities

Improve relationship within the organization

And more

FACILITATION

Strategic Planning

Team Building with Staff and/or Board

Meetings

SEMINARS

Leadership

Board of Directors Development

Fundraising

Donor and Volunteer Stewardship